Our Family Record Book

Contents

Our Amazing Family

Our crazy, happy, loud and loving family are everything. We live together, eat together, go out and stay in together, fight and have fun together. It's good to have a family you can rely on, who'll accept you for who you are, help you out, and care for you if you're down. Wherever we are, whatever is happening, we'll always have each other.

Our Family Tree

Our family tree draws together the links between us, our immediate family, our extended family and our ancestors.

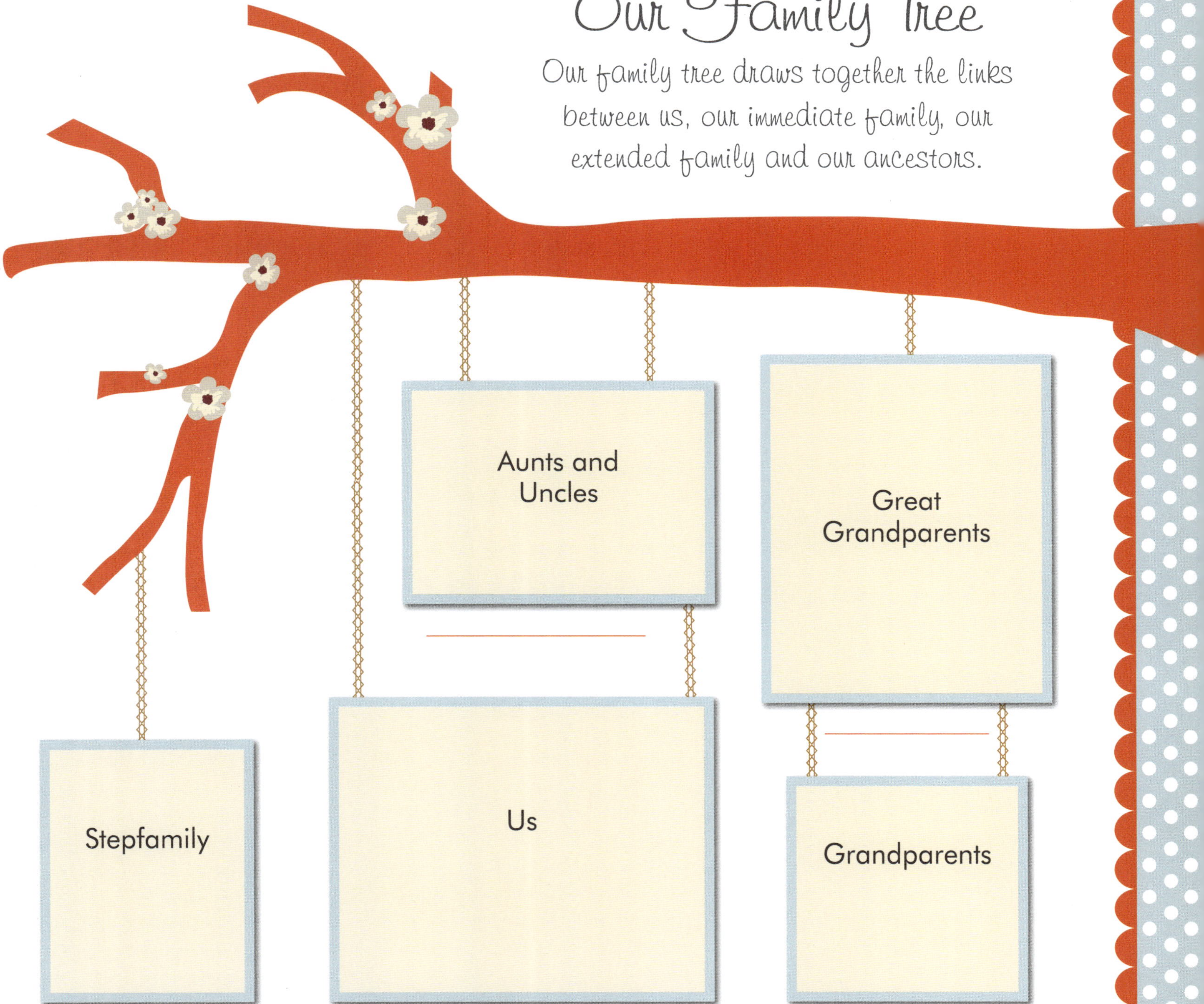

About Mum

I have so many names that reflect who I am, but Mum is my favourite. Once a mum, always a mum.

Name:

Date of birth:

Place of birth:

Hair and eye colour:

Personality:

Favourite Mum photo here

Favourite Things:

Mum's family photo back then

About Dad

Being a dad, my first priority
is my family. Everything I really
care about is right there.

Name:

Date of birth:

Place of birth:

Hair and eye colour:

Personality:

Favourite Dad
photo here

Favourite Things:

Dad's family
photo back then

Sons

Life would be so dull without the boisterous energy of sons and step-sons. They liven up our days.

Name:

Date of birth:

Place of birth:

Hair and eye colour:

Personality:

Favourite Things:

Our favourite photo of son

Our favourite photo of son

Name:

Date of birth:

Place of birth:

Hair and eye colour:

Personality:

Favourite Things:

Son's favourite photo of himself

Our favourite photo of son

Daughters

Daughters and step-daughters
are a true delight. They bring a ray
of sunshine into all our lives.

Name:

Date of birth:

Place of birth:

Hair and eye colour:

Personality:

Favourite Things:

Our favourite
photo of daughter

Our favourite
photo of daughter

Name:

Date of birth:

Place of birth:

Hair and eye colour:

Personality:

Favourite Things:

Our favourite photo of daughter

Daughter's favourite photo of herself

Grandparents

When Mum's mum and dad come to see us, they make us all feel very special.

Grandma's name:

Date of birth:

Place of birth:

All about Grandma:

Grandad's name:

Date of birth:

Place of birth:

All about Grandad:

Photo of Mum's parents

Fond memories:

Grandparents

Dad's mum and dad have a fund of great stories about days gone by.

Photo of Dad's parents

Grandma's name:

Date of birth:

Place of birth:

All about Grandma:

Fond memories:

Grandad's name:

Date of birth:

Place of birth:

All about Grandad:

Aunts and Uncles

It's good to meet up with extended family, catch up on news and remember good times together.

Aunts:

The family together

Uncles:

Cousins

We love it when we get together with our cousins. We have so much in common!

Cousins:

Peas in a pod

Practically Family

There are special people
in our lives who are not related,
but still count as family.

Name:

How we know them:

One of us

Name:

How we know them:

Name:

How we know them:

True stories:

So close!

Pets

We love our pets and care for them.
They are part of our family.
It wouldn't be the same without them.

Name:

Type of animal:

Description:

Best toy:

Favourite game:

Fondest memories:

Our favourite photo of our pet

Our favourite photo of our pet

Name:

Type of animal:

Description:

Best toy:

Favourite game:

Fondest memories:

Here are some of our best pet photos.
Some are cute, some make us giggle
and some make us so proud!

So clever!

Awkward!

Relax!

Paws for thought

So cute!

Our Happy Home

It's not what you have that makes a happy home, it's who you have sharing it. That said, it doesn't harm to have a few rules to keep things running smoothly. There are some things we can all agree on: sharing is a good thing; everyone needs their own space once in a while; the refrigerator is the beating heart of the home…

Our House

Our house is just like us.
It may not suit everyone, but for us,
it is the best place in the world.

When we moved in:

Best bits:

Whose Room?

There'll be no points for guessing which room is which! I think we can all figure that one out...

The heart of the home:

The kitchen

Sitting room

The family room:

Do not disturb:

Bedroom

Bedroom

Knock first:

House Rules

Amid the chaos, there are
house rules to keep us sane.
If only we'd all stick to them!

Rule 1:

Rule 2:

Rule 3:

Rule 4:

Rule 5:

Rule 6:

Rule 7:

Rule 8:

House Rules

- Be polite
- Take turns
- Listen
- No fighting
- No shouting
- No running indoors
- Tell the truth
- Help out
- Share

A Typical Day in the Life of Us

Every day is a new adventure but there are some things we can count on. Here are some of the things we do daily together that make up our family life.

How we get up and out of the house:

What we all do all day:

Mealtimes:

Sharing the day's news

Family time

How we spend our evenings:

A typical week in the life of us

Between us all, it's busy, busy, busy. We are constantly on the go.
A little routine helps us keep track of what's happening.

Monday:

Tuesday:

Wednesday:

Thursday:

Life on the go

Friday:

Saturday:

Sunday:

Sharing Chores

A family works best when everyone pulls together. So we all take turns and share the chores.

Washing the dishes:

Cooking:

Vacuuming:

Taking out the rubbish:

Doing the laundry:

Making the beds:

Feeding the pets:

Watering the plants:

To Do List

Family Fortunes

What's in a name? Well, there's a story behind every family name. First names are chosen, it's just a matter of finding out who chose which name and why. Surnames connect us with our ancestors. Who knows, we may even find a family crest!

Family Names

Surnames can tell you where the family came from, what kind of jobs they did and even what your ancestors looked like!

Our surname:

Our first names:

Name:
Meaning:
Named after:
Nicknames:

Name:
Meaning:
Named after:
Nicknames:

Name:
Meaning:
Named after:
Nicknames:

Name:
Meaning:
Named after:
Nicknames:

Name:
Meaning:
Named after:
Nicknames:

Name:
Meaning:
Named after:
Nicknames:

Family Traits

It could be the way you laugh, a quirky walk or a shared talent – there are family traits we recognise in each other.

It's a family thing

Best traits:

Worst traits:

Something we all share:

Family Rituals

Every family has a few habits that seem a bit weird to outsiders. They help to build family bonds.

The way we do things:

Family sayings:

Our favourite family ritual

Things we like to do together

There are so many activities that we love to do together – watching a film, going out for a picnic, playing games or looking at photo albums.

Make and do:

Outings:

Games:

Sports:

Collecting:

Treasure hunt

A fine feat

Exploring:

Playing:

Who won?

Guess who?

Dressing up:

Lending a hand:

Good job!

Surprise!

Visiting:

Family Calendar

January

February

March

April

May

June

July

August

September

October

November

December

Family Timeline

Our family timeline shows landmark events and life-changing moments in our lives. From bringing our first baby home to waving our last child off to their independence and greeting them again with their own growing families. There are so many special episodes to our own family soap opera.

From the beginning...

This timeline shows landmark events and life-changing moments in our lives.

Date	Event Details

Date	Event Details

Date	Event Details

Date	Event Details

Date	Event Details

Date	Event Details

Date	Event Details

Date	Event Details

Date	Event Details

Date	Event Details

Date	Event Details

Date	Event Details

Date	Event Details

Date	Event Details

Date	Event Details

Date	Event Details

Date	Event Details

Date	Event Details

Memory Lane

This fabulous family is constantly growing and changing. It's so easy to forget how far we have all come. Family portraits capture precious moments and freeze them in time, helping us to preserve those special memories.

Do you remember when?

There are so many random memories that sum up our family life. Here are some of them.

We'll never forget:

Earliest family photo

Family Portraits

Here are some photos that mark important events and celebrations in our lives.

Mother and daughter

Father and son

Inseparable

So proud!

We are heroes

Best day ever

Fun Family Portraits

Awkward, embarrassing, daft or caught on camera – some photos remind us that family life has its sillier moments!

Daddy's little helper

Mummy's angel

Funny at the time

Little treasure

Oops!

Candid

The gang

Friends forever

Hugs

Epic Holidays

What happens when the whole family decamps for the holidays, dumps the everyday routine and throws caution to the wind? It's epic!

Where:

When:

What we did:

Where:

When:

What we did:

Where:

When:

What we did:

Where:

When:

What we did:

Where:

When:

What we did:

What happened next...

Legend!

Where:

When:

What we did:

Where:

When:

What we did:

Never seen anything like it!

So much fun!

Where:

When:

What we did:

Where:

When:

What we did:

Fabulous

Unforgettable

Where:

When:

What we did:

Family Christmas

Whatever happens during the year, Christmas
is always a highlight. Nobody is too young or too
old to join in the excitement of Christmas,

Decorating our home:

Christmas treats:

Letter to Santa:

Visit to Santa:

Nativity play:

Santa's been!

Best Christmas
tree ever

Night before Christmas:

Christmas wake-up call:

Christmas angels

'Tis the season to be jolly

Present opening:

Christmas dinner:

I spy Santa!

Who's a Christmas turkey?

Christmas traditions:

Special Events

Birthday, anniversaries, engagements, weddings – there are so many wonderful family events that bring us all together.

Good times!

Family affair

Congratulations!

Happy Birthday!

Proud parents

The happy couple

Happy families

Soulmates

Notes

PULTENEY PRESS

First published by Pulteney Press in 2017

Written by Katherine Sully

ISBN 978-1-78718-689-7

Printed in China